The Customer Is Always Right

And 7½ Other Outdated Myths Which Are Destroying Your Beauty Business

ISBN: 978-1-9162472-0-8

First published 2019

Disclaimer

For Hollie.
Thank you for believing in me, supporting my dreams and always being there... even through the dark times and the silly ideas.
xx

Contents

Introduction

Business is difficult, but I have good news.

You've already done the hardest bit. Taking the leap is the most difficult step and the one which 99% of people will never even attempt.

So give yourself a pat on the back and congratulate yourself. You are amazing. Seriously.

Why did you decide to go into business for yourself? I always knew that I one day I would own my own business. Or businesses, as it's turned out.

Not because I didn't think I'd be a good employee either, as is the case with many people. I was a damned good employee for several companies before I took my almighty plunge into the unknown. Mostly because I wanted the freedom which I thought came with owning your own business.

Work the hours I choose. Work with whom I wanted to. Have as much free time as I liked so that I can do the other things I enjoy.

Thing is, it didn't always work out like that.

There is so much that people never tell you about running your own business. Like the bit about working every hour we are sent. Or the bit about all of the unexpected costs. Or what happens when new competition sets up on your doorstep. Or even the sheer hilarity of payroll, taxes and submitting your accounts.

This book isn't about those things. You can, and will, learn to cope with those twists and turns along your journey. This book is about something which can be even more damaging.

It's about the things that people *do* tell you about running your own business. Things which I've since learned aren't necessarily true. Even though many people believe they are. Like goldfish having three second memories.

(Admit it, you just Googled that, didn't you? They don't, if you're interested, and actually have pretty good memory function).

Answer me this; what has been your source for your business learning up until now?

Your friends and family? Common parlance and hearsay? A textbook written in 1990? What some friendly stranger in a coffee shop once told you? Mimicking what your competition are doing?

You see, all of that *might* be fine.

Assuming of course that those imparting their wisdom on you already have the results which you want. But if they don't, then shouldn't you at least find out for yourself if what they say is *actually* true?

Everyone likes to think they are an expert because they watched a TV show on a subject once or read a magazine article or blog post.

Truth is that many of the people you might have listened to in the past don't even own their own businesses - let alone have successful businesses in the same industry as yours.

Maybe it's time you changed your set of reference? Start here, with this book.

I'm not going to be so arrogant as to claim I have all the answers. But what I do know is that in my role as a beauty business success coach and mentor I've spoken with hundreds of small business owners just like you.

And it turns out that lots of them have a certain set of beliefs, ideas and assumptions. You might have some of them too.

I want to challenge them - and if you agree with me then I'd encourage you to change your way of thinking too and start implanting some of the ideas in your business. Who knows where you might end up?

Maybe even finally having the business of your dreams and satisfying every last reason why you got into this in the first place.

Success leaves tracks. The time to start following them is now. I'll even hold your hand.

Let's begin.

Ryan

1. Newsletters

If you ask my wife she'll agree that lots of things irritate me. Badly behaved children, men with top knots and dog owners who fail to pick up their precious pooch's poop all make the cut.

However, close to the top of that particular list of irritants are newsletters.

I *hate* newsletters.

What I hate even more than newsletters is how commonplace they've become. That's why for some time now I've been leading a one man crusade against their continued widespread popularity.

I understand why so many people have them on their websites. After all, many of the large retailers have them. We've all been bombarded with them on a regular basis from the likes of Boots and Sainsbury's. Besides, your web designer may also have told you they are an essential part of your website.

However, they aren't. They suck.

Now I don't want you to misunderstand where I'm coming from here. Collecting your website visitor's email address is a wonderful idea, in fact I'll go as far as declaring it essential. It's what you do with that information moving forward which annoys me. Sending a newsletter is a shocking waste of this resource.

Allow me to explain why — as well as giving you a much better strategy which you can employ with far greater ease, with much less cost and effort and one which will not only delight your future clients but will build your relationship with them before they even step foot into your premises.

Let's take it back a few steps first.

I hope that I don't have to explain to you why you need a website for your business. A website has been a must have for businesses of every size and shape for probably twenty years now.

I'm going to assume you have one. (If you don't then you really should consider investing in one sooner rather than later — see the appendices for a few suggestions).

So your website is out there on the internet attracting visitors from any number of means. Maybe people have searched you out on the internet intentionally, maybe they've never heard of you and stumbled across your site, perhaps they've been passed your business card from a friend or have even been recommended to you via a search engine. It matters not. Point is, they've found you. They could have landed on any number of other websites but there they are, eagerly consuming yours.

Now I hate to break the bad news to you but the chances are that they'll take no action after landing on your site whatsoever. Unless you include clicking back from wherever they came.

That's just how it is. 99% of your website traffic will disappear again into the abyss. Most of them won't make an enquiry, a booking or a purchase. Most of them won't even watch that video or read that blog which took you hours to write. Some might, sure, but most won't.

And to think how much effort you put in getting them there, just for them to leave again. Heck, you may have even *paid* to get them there after they clicked on your advert somewhere. And they *still* didn't take any action. What a bummer!

So wouldn't it be great if you had some way of continuing the conversation with them? You see just because they didn't take some action right then doesn't necessarily mean they won't in the future.

They may have just got distracted. (The internet is full of distractions, in case you hadn't noticed).

One of the best ways to continue that conversation with them is via email. Broadly speaking it's free, you can automate lots of it and you can build relationships using it. Marvellous.

Now comes the step where people get it wrong. They pop a little message on the website with a couple of boxes and some text which reads something along the lines of '*Subscribe to our newsletter here*'.

Wrong, diddly-wrong-wrong.

Firstly, most people don't care about your news and they sure as hell don't care about your newsletter.

They don't even know you yet, so why would they? I personally don't care about the 'news' from companies I know, trust and even love so I sure as hell don't about a business I have no association with at all.

Your potential clients will feel the same.

There is also something else going on here. People see 'newsletter' and think 'thinly veiled attempt to sell me something'. People aren't going to welcome that into their inbox with open arms either.

Furthermore, people are far more guarded with their emails now. The average person receives 144 emails per day now. 144!

That's a lot of email. They don't want more, most probably. Unless it's good. Really good. And newsletters don't fall into that category. They fall into the category of 'generally left unopened and borderline irritating'.

Answer this honestly; are there any newsletters you receive from other businesses which you can't wait to open? Ones where you think, "gee that's late this month, I wonder what's happened?"

Heck, no! (And if there is, I'd love to know who sends that newsletter and what they are doing so wildly differently to everyone else).

So we've established that people don't really want to receive them. Let's assume that for some odd reason some people have still signed up for yours (as of course, most people won't bother). Sadly the problems don't end there.

For some strange reason someone somewhere once educated the world that the best way to design a newsletter is with flashing banners, large and colourful images and all different fonts and logos. Let's be clear, this is a terrible way to design them.

Not only are the majority ghastly but even those beautifully crafted by the world's greatest designers still slip up.

This is because most email providers have spam filters on them. Pretty good ones too, for the most part. They know a newsletter when they see one. And they treat them with the disdain which they deserve.

Those pretty images? Yeah, they probably won't load properly (if at all) and will look terrible. Although that won't matter too much of course as nobody will ever see them as they prop up the recipient's junk folder.

These emails are considered as promotional (even if you're not promoting anything) and will be filed away for nothing more than dust collecting duties in the promotion, spam or junk folders.

Let's play devil's advocate for a moment and assume that some of your newsletters are making it through the filters and arrive in the inbox. What then? Well to begin with, of course, most of them won't get opened or read. Largely because people put something in the subject line such as 'September Newsletter' and we've already established that most people don't give a hoot about your news!

(Please, don't be too despondent here, as they actually don't care about *anyone's* news other than their own, but more on that later).

So, what's the solution? Well to begin with you need to give them something they actually want. Something which they'll happily exchange their email address for *and* feel like they've done well out of the deal to boot.

In an ideal world you want to offer something which solves a problem for your reader. And when I say reader you should have your dream client in mind as you consider what this problem and solution might be.

What are the biggest problems which your dream clients face?

Of course, this is going to depend on who your target market are and which section of the industry you serve.

But you should know what these problems are already. Your current clients will have already told you. I hope you were listening. What questions do you get continually asked? What solutions are they looking for? What are the real pain points which keep your existing clients awake at night?

These questions should point you in the right direction. Perhaps they all want to know how to keep their skin looking youthful. Maybe they want to know how they can maintain that 'fresh from the salon' look for longer. Or how they can prevent chipped nails for longer. It'll vary from business to business but hopefully you've already got a few ideas buzzing around your head.

You now need to turn those problems into a solution for your clients. Or, moreover, your future clients whom you've not even met yet. Your future business depends on them.

Here comes an important point, which I'll repeat in case you missed it earlier.

Ready?

Your clients don't care about you, they only care about themselves.

They will constantly be thinking, "yeah, but what's in it for me?" That may sound like a really negative way to view the world but in marketing terms at least it's entirely true. Keep that in mind, always.

The good news is that by identifying their problems — and then solving them for them — they are going to love you. Before they've even met you. Furthermore not only are they going to love you but some of them are also going to become regular paying clients. A few might even bring their friends to see you, too. Oh, rejoice!

So you've identified the problem which they want solved. The next step is to solve it for them. This may sound tricky at first but actually it's very simple because you're the expert in your field and they aren't.

A great way to solve their problem is with a checklist of ideas, tips or even 'insider secrets' which they'll be keen to learn. First, think of as many ways to solve the problem as you can. Ask some of your colleagues and do some additional research if you need to. Even though you're going to give this advice away for free, a good rule of thumb is to make it good enough that people would gladly pay their hard earned cash for it.

If you have an odd number of ideas, tips or secrets then fab. If you have an even number then get rid of the weakest one. Ensure your list is an odd number of between 3 and 11 items. (Don't ask me the reasons why on this but loads of psychology studies have shown these numbers to be far more appealing to us as humans).

Now you've a decision to make. You want to either turn these tips into a video (or short video series, if you're really comfortable on camera) or an ebook.

If you've just started heavily panting and are approaching hot flush territory then relax. It's mercifully easy, I promise.

Now if you're comfortable on a camera then do this; simply shoot a short video (or a series of them if you've lots of content) running through the top tips. Don't start promoting your business or anything like that, it's too early.

The point of the videos is to enhance your position as an authority on the subject and to build massive goodwill with your future clients. This is about them and their problem, remember? Not you. They don't care about you. Yet.

Videos can even be shot on your iPhone. No need to hire a videographer (unless you really want to) as the technology of the day which we are blessed with is more than enough. Just make sure that you use a tripod and that you're well lit.

The videos should be no more than 5 minutes each in length. Short, sharp and to the point. Give the viewer what they are after as succinctly as possible. It's then simply a matter of uploading these to YouTube so that you can send the links to your soon-to-be new fans.

If you can get a little personality in there then all the better, and indeed this is one of the key advantages which video has over the written word. If people can see you then they are far more likely to trust and like you.

It's worth adding at this point that people buy people. What that means is that if someone likes you already from watching your videos and comes in to see you then they are way more likely to do business with you. Fact.

If you like the idea of video but don't have the necessary means to record it, edit it or whatever then you could always consider outsourcing the bits you can't do. It needn't be expensive either if you use one of the many websites which offer such services (again, see the appendices for some suggestions). If you do, just make sure that you choose experienced freelancers who have a good feedback on the website you choose.

OK, so what if you don't want — or aren't able — to record your tips on video.

That's not a problem... you can become a published author instead!

This is even easier. Compile your same list of tips, hints or secrets into a short document on Word. No more than 3-5 pages works best. Again, you're not selling anything here you're just giving value. Massive value. The 'best stuff you have got' type of value.

You'll then want to give your new book a catchy title. This is a very important step, so please don't rush this. You'll want to mention the pain point your future client is feeling as well as letting them know that you've got the solution for them.

You'll also want to include the number of tips, hints or secrets which you have as people will be drawn to this. Think newspaper headlines and you'll be on the right tracks. Some examples might include;

Still Suffering With Spots?
7 Insider Secrets Which The Big Brands Don't Want You To Hear

Dull Hair?
These 5 Ideas You Can Do At Home Will Bring
Your Locks Back To Life - And Will Cost You No More Than Pennies!

On Fleek! The 9 Nail Trends For This Year
Which Your Friends Don't Even Know About

Hopefully you get the idea. Think eye catching, red-top tabloid newspaper journalism. Remember you don't have long to pull your reader in and capture their email address so it needs to be attention grabbing, play to their pain points and possibly even provocate.

Now Word documents are great, but you now need to turn this into a guide which someone would pay more money for. You're not going to charge them anything but try to make it look good enough that someone would.

If you're a whizz on computers then you can do it yourself and convert your file to a PDF which can be easily delivered via email.

If not then you can get a nice one designed for you (including one of those fancy 3D book cover images you've no doubt seen before) for less than £20. That's a total bargain and will have paid for itself the first time someone comes and sees you after reading it.

Now you're ready to go! I told you it was simple.

All you need to do now is have an automated system for delivery of your guide or video. Next, if you have a newsletter already then this will replace that. You simply have a form on your website (every page of your website, ideally) which people can drop their name and email address into in exchange for your guide or video.

They then receive an email — which you've written in advance, you don't write one every time — with a link to whatever they've signed up for.

Now this is really simple with much of the automated email software used today. I recommend ConvertKit as it's awesome and inexpensive (see https://salonology.uk/convertkit for a free trial) but there are plenty of others you can use, including MailChimp, Aweber, Active Campaign and more.

You might need your web geek to make your website and your email software talk to each other but it should be a very quick, simple and inexpensive job for them. We're talking fifteen minutes tops if they know what they're doing.

So you now have your guide ready to be delivered on autopilot to your prospective new clients. However, this is only half of the challenge and I want to bring you back to the original point of this chapter.

Once they've joined your email database (and you'll need them to jump through a few compliance hoops first — again, your web geek can help you here) then it's important that you don't just continue to send them newsletters! That is what we're trying to get away from here!

Now it's worth bearing in mind at this point that now you've got something in place which people actually want (how many people were signing up for your newsletter every week, anyway?), you can expect your list to grow at a far greater pace.

The subject of how to send good emails which actually make you money is probably large enough to write a standalone book on but I will cover some of the basics here for you. Anything to stop you sending those damned email newsletters…

To begin with I want you to start sending emails written in plain text. That means no more fancy fonts. That means no more flashing anything. That means all written in the same easy to read font, in black and all in the same size. That means extremely limited use of photos, if at all.

Basically you want the email to look — at first glance — pretty dull. I know, I know.

You're thinking that doesn't make any sense but please bear with me on this.

I want you to now have a little think about the emails which you enjoy receiving. Is it those flashy all singing and all dancing ones from the big retailers. Or is it those short ones you receive from your friends? You know, the ones which are written in a normal style, without some flashy email editor, without the flashing doo-dahs. The ones where they've probably just hit 'compose' or 'reply' and then started typing.

I thought so. That's the style of emails you're going to send from now on. Emails which look — and read — as though they've been sent from one friend to another.

Emails which take a conversational tone and read as though they've been written from one person to one person. None of this 'dear reader' nonsense or any implications whatsoever that the email is being sent to hundreds (or even thousands) of other people.

Make the reader think that you're writing to an audience of one. Them. Make them feel special. Let them know that you care about them and their problems.

People don't care how much you know until they know how much you care.

Eventually, with time, your readers will start to enjoy your messages, trust you and feel that they even know you. Don't be afraid to email personal stories and open up a little to them. It'll bring them closer toward you.

You want to move away from the cold, hard newsletter and think more along the lines of an affectionate note passed between good friends. It's essential that you send them regularly — aim for one per week — and keep them short, simple and conversational.

You'll find that people start to email you back, something I'll bet seldom happens after you send your newsletters out currently.

When they do then you know you're doing it right. It means that people are interested in what you've said and that they believe you've only sent the email to them. (Which of course you haven't, you've used your clever email software to send the same thing to everyone).

You can even continue to use some of the information you'd have sent out in your old newsletter in your new emails. You are just delivering it in a different way.

Break it all up into smaller messages and make it more personable. Remember that your reader probably doesn't care about much of it, unless it impacts them and their needs. If it's all you, you, you then consider scrapping it and starting again.

The ironic thing is that once you have this system in place you'll realise that the emails are far easier to send, will come much more naturally to you (remember, it's just like the emails you currently send to all of your friends anyway) and you'll get some positive results off the back of it.

When you take someone on the journey from having never heard of you, to reading your ebook, to opening your emails, to coming and trying your salon out for the first time then it's a wonderful feeling.

You can enjoy it soon, too. Start by brainstorming some ideas today.

2. Getting Your Name Out There With Brand Awareness

You know when Christmas is just around the corner.

The festive songs begin to grace the radio stations. The big retailers change their window displays. And, of course, you get *that* advert rammed down your throat. You know the one. "The holidays are coming…"

Yup, pretty much the biggest brand awareness campaign ever.

What exactly Coca-Cola has to do with the biggest Christian holiday of the year I've never quite figured out.

But they sure do want to be associated with it, that much I know. From as far back as the 1930's Coca-Cola's depiction of good ol' Father Christmas has been as the jolly, bearded character with a red and white suit which children everywhere still know, love, write to and even leave mince pies out for. Bless.

Not satisfied with this, however, Coca-Cola also see fit to have their own song about it, some giant trucks which tour the globe and, of course, *that* advert which is seemingly played on loop from mid-October onwards.

So, why do they do it? Does it sell them a lot more Coca-Cola? Well the irony of the whole matter is that I don't know. And I doubt that Coca-Cola do, either. And therein lies the problem.

This type of brand awareness campaign is expensive. Like, really expensive. And additionally, as just mentioned, it's difficult to tell if it even works or not. So whilst that might be fine if you're the biggest soft drink manufacturer on the planet, it's probably not such a good fit if you're a mobile nail tech in Dartford.

Coca-Cola has an outrageous position in the marketplace. 3% of all drinks consumed everyday worldwide are from the Coca-Cola family. Their name has even become a verb, much like Google has. They bring in almost $42 billion per year in net sales revenue.

However their annual advertising budget is around $4 billion per year. (Yes, with a 'b'). And to think they've little way of testing if a lot of that works or not.

I would recommend that you don't run brand awareness campaigns. Like, never. As there is a better way. But first, a story.

Where I live is a real hot-spot for barbers. I have no idea why but there are four or five all within a few hundred yards of each other in our local parade of shops. I'm not sure there is necessarily the demand to keep them *all* busy but I do take some interest in seeing which are busy as I pass them and what they are each doing to stay ahead of one another. Sadly most of them do precious little. And by little, I actually mean nothing.

So imagine my delight when one morning I came home to discover a little surprise waiting on my doormat. Behold - a leaflet from one of the barbers!

Wow, now this really was something. Some actual pro-active marketing. There I was — a local man, with all my own hair — stood reading their literature. Imagine how many others in the neighbouring houses and streets were doing the same? Quite a few, most probably.

Now the leaflet sadly wasn't the best. But, importantly, it was much, much better than no leaflet at all. Done is always better than perfect. (You might want to jot that one down or commit it to memory).

Really all the leaflet did was tell me where the shop was and that they 'specialise' in the same thing most barbers claim to. Cutting hair, for the most part.

There was no real call to action, no special offer to entice me to come and visit, not even a nod to their social media page. But I thought I'd go and pay them a visit next time I needed a trim, all the same. So, when the time came, I decide to visit the barber who had leaflet dropped my house.

We get chatting about marketing (once we'd ticked off critical opinions on football, the weather and what I was doing that weekend of course). I ask what he finds works well for him. After a bit of '*um*'-ing and '*ah*'-ing I realise that he doesn't really know. He has pretty much no idea where the customers who walk into his shop are coming from.

He isn't even aware that I've had one of his leaflets through my door and that's why I'm sat in a silly cloak talking to him via a mirror. I asked if he'd ever tried a leaflet drop.

"*Well*", he started, "*we tried it once but didn't get much. Still, they're good for getting your name out there.*"

Coca-Cola can afford to 'get their name out there' and hope that some of it sticks. As small business owners, we can't. Nor should we want to, anyway. There is a better way of course and I'm going to explain it right now for you.

All of the marketing you ever do should be based on the principles of 'direct response marketing'. If you've not heard that term before, then here's a little definition for you. According to techopedia.com;

"Direct response marketing is a type of marketing that elicits a specific, measured response resulting from a consumer's direct response to a marketer. Direct response marketing facilitates the delivery of a call to action and outcome via direct or online interaction for immediate feedback and response."*

So what does that mean? Well it means structuring your adverts and marketing materials in such a way so that you can determine afterwards whether or not they've been a success.

Let's go back to the leaflets as an example. Let's pretend that my barber paid £100 to get his leaflets designed and printed and to save a little bit of money he bribed his teenage son to deliver them all for him in exchange for taxi services rendered.

So we know that he has paid out £100 so far. Now the real question is how much money have the leaflets brought back in? How much cash for the business has his marketing exercise generated?

Well the answer, of course, is I don't know. Nor do you. And, rather tragically, nor does my barber. Because he has no way of accurately knowing.

Had my barber adopted a direct response marketing approach then he would have a lot more information at his fingertips. He might also have a few more people in his shop!

Here's how I'd have done it differently.

I'd have still tried a leaflet drop campaign. It's a crowded marketplace so done correctly it could be a good way to stand out a little and get his message in my hands. Also, he has a potential customer (or maybe more) in almost every single house so you'd expect to pick up some new clients and maybe also bring a few older ones back along the way.

Now, here's where I'd change it up a little. The next stage should be to construct some form of enticement. Something to make people actually want to take some action. The ideal action, of course, being going and getting a haircut. Like, now.

In a perfect world this enticement should be offered only to those holding a leaflet. Make it exclusive. Make the client feel special. Put a little effort and imagination in, too. A free beard tidy or one minute scalp massage with every haircut is much better than 5% off the price.

Here comes the kicker; to get the offer they have to bring the leaflet back to you or quote the unique code which you've printed on the leaflet.

Then you'll know — with absolute certainty — how many sales you can attribute to that leaflet drop. Whilst not rocket science, it is effective. It will also save you a lot of money.

So not only will this leaflet appeal to far more clients than a generic and bland one which just lists all the things he does, but means he can actually test its effectiveness too. That's a win-win right there.

At the end of the month he'll be able to see how many sales of his 'beard tidy exclusive' were achieved and what those sales are worth to him.

Then he can determine whether it's worth getting more leaflets printed and distributed. If he only had two clients then it probably wouldn't be worth it. But if he had 50 then maybe he should send his son out every week!

Can you see how this direct marketing system outperforms the blanket approach for small businesses like ours?

Do you know where all of your clients are coming from? Which specific adverts on which specific platforms are making you money and which are losing you money?

If you're unsure then now is the time to start adopting this approach in your marketing. And it doesn't only apply to leaflets, either. You can use this approach for the vast majority of your marketing output.

There are several ways in which you can track where your clients are coming from and some are better than others.

Personally I find asking people to be one of the worst. People forget, they are bombarded with marketing messages from everyone under the sun all day long and they'll likely give you the first thing they think of. Or the top one in the list you provide!

Instead, you should either ask them for a specific code so that they can claim your exclusive offer or you should send them to a specific webpage or telephone number which is unique to that advert.

The simplest way to do this is to have a unique code they've got to quote. You see this on TV and hear it on radio adverts all the time. "*Make sure you quote TV26 to get your free eight month bonus supply of essential vitamins with your Ab-Cruncher 8000 whilst stocks last…*" or whatever.

They do this so that at the end of the promotion they can see which code performed best. They most likely have a different advert code for each advert or each channel it's broadcast on. Probably both.

You can do the same, very easily, for your business.

You must keep a log of all the codes you've used and where you've used them. You then just log all of the sales which are attributed to them. This is easy when the client has to use the code to claim whatever you're enticing them in with.

If you're doing it online then it's even easier. One option is to get your web geeks to set up different landing pages for each advert (the content on the pages is the same, just the web address different so that you can track visits). So you might have pages such as www.hairdresser.co.uk/tv1 and then another www.hairdresser.co.uk/leaflet1 and so on.

You can even do this with telephones too, if you want people to call you as opposed to visit your website. In this instance you need what are called tracking numbers and the good news is they are as cheap as chips these days!

So you would literally give a different telephone number in each of your ads. Of course, the same physical phone rings regardless of which number is called so it makes no difference to your clients.

Then, at the month end you'll get a report from your telephone company telling you which numbers were dialled most frequently to get through to you.

Ta-da! You now know exactly which ads are making your phone ring and which aren't.

As a final point it's worth noting here that you want to ensure that you include one very strong, and very obvious call to action in each marketing piece you ever create. This means directly instructing the client with what you want them to do next. Don't leave it to chance, tell them what you want to them do to - and then make that really easy for them.

If you want them to phone you then state that, very clearly, with the telephone number you want them to call along with a wonderful reason as to why they should do so right now. Make it a total no-brainer for them.

Don't rely on people finding your number or your website for themselves. People are lazy and get easily bored and distracted. Some of them won't ever get around to it. Remove the chance element and make it simple for them.

Commit right now to adding a direct response to your next advert. At least that way you'll know whether it was worth running the advert or not…

3. Relying On Too Few Marketing Pillars

Athena — the ancient Greek goddess of wisdom, handicraft and warfare was a revered lady.

So much so, in fact, that she had numerous buildings, temples and monuments dedicated to her in ancient Greece. None more spectacular — or still culturally relevant — than the Parthenon.

If you've never been then you're probably familiar with the image (it's the one on the hill with the massive stone pillars). Despite being built nearly 2,500 years ago it still stands today. Quite incredible when you think about it.

So, what's the relevance of this to your business? Not due to my love of history, I can assure you, but rather because your business is very similar to this historical temple. Let me explain.

The reason the temple still stands today — and how it survived Athens being attacked multiple times throughout history — is due to its giant pillars. Had there only been two pillars then no doubt the building would no longer be standing. But there weren't only two. There were 46 outer columns and 23 inner columns and therefore she's still going strong.

Your business is like the Parthenon. It too is reliant on pillars to keep it upright; standing tall, thriving and surviving as various competitors try to knock it down.

Within your business each pillar is a way to promote your business, or source of attracting clients into your business, which you currently use.

Some are free and some can be very expensive. They might also be referred to as marketing streams, channels or sources.

There are plenty to choose from and with technology moving at its current rate even more will probably have sprung up in the time taken for me to finish this book.

This, therefore, won't be an exhaustive list but here are just a few ways that you could market your business if you chose to.

Make a note of how many you've tried…

- Facebook business page
- Dedicated Facebook group
- Facebook paid advertising
- Facebook messenger advertising
- Instagram business profile
- Instagram advertisting
- Snapchat profile
- Snapchat paid advertising
- Twitter business page
- Twitter paid advertising
- LinkedIn profiles
- LinkedIn advertising
- YouTube channel
- YouTube advertising
- Google search sponsored adverts
- Google display adverts
- Google retargeting adverts
- Google My Business listing
- Search engine optimisation
- Yell and other directory site listings (both paid and free)

- Local listing sites and link exchanges with other local businesses
- Contribute to local online forums and websites
- Ebay, Gumtree and other listings sites
- Your own website
- Discount vouchers or codes
- Affiliate marketing schemes (other people selling for you)
- Writing a blog
- Contributing to someone else's blog
- Starting a podcast
- Contributing to someone else's podcast
- Email marketing
- Email signatures
- Advertising space on other people's emails
- Mobile app
- Posters for your window and others' windows
- Distribute flyers through local residents doors
- Billboards
- A-board outside your premises
- Put adverts on local noticeboards (think supermarkets and Post Offices)
- Radio advertising
- Get on a local radio show as a guest expert
- Television (local television is a good place to start)
- Networking events
- Exhibitions and conferences
- Speak at an event
- Hold your own open night or VIP event
- Wedding shows
- Sponsor or contribute to a local charity event

- Enter some award ceremonies
- Run a competition
- Testimonials and case studies
- Word of mouth
- Referral schemes
- VIP client schemes
- Loyalty programmes
- Business cards (including loading up friends and family to distribute for you!)
- Advertising wrap for your car
- Give away car stickers (as radio stations do)
- Send your clients something in the post
- Send your clients birthday cards
- Send your clients thank you cards
- Telephone your clients to invite them back in
- Text messages
- WhatsApp
- Upselling and cross-selling additional products and treatments
- Newspaper and magazine adverts
- Newspaper and magazine editorial pieces
- Press releases
- Banner adverts on other business'websites
- Branded clothing
- Branded merchandise (which could be given away for free, not necessarily sold)
- Write a book (or at least an ebook)
- Customer surveys (to existing or potential future clients)

Okay, so there were seventy or so ideas which you could try in your business.

Now — and answer this honestly - how many have you tried?

And I'm talking about properly tested here to see if they worked for you. Not a little pathetic toe-dip to see how cold the water is.

You see, what works for one company won't necessarily work for another. What works for me might need to be tweaked for you.

That's one reason why you need to test new ideas. *Lots* of new ideas. There are plenty more reasons, too.

One of the most important reasons is that sectors of the market will respond differently from one type of media to another. Not only will they respond differently but there's every chance you'll miss people altogether relying on only a few pillars.

So you might get your message in front of one client using social media but to get the same message in front of her mother then you might need a local newspaper advert — and to get in front of *her* mother then maybe a message board advert in the Post Office, perhaps!

So if you want to attract more clients then you need to start trying some new marketing pillars.

Don't be so naive as to think that "everyone is on Facebook, so that's all I need". Sure, Facebook can be a part of your overall strategy, that would be smart. Just don't rely entirely on it. Firstly, not everyone is on Facebook. Secondly, not everyone is looking at it every five minutes (even if you are) and thirdly you really don't want to be reliant on someone else's website for all of your clients.

What happens if Facebook change their algorithm again? Or double their advertising costs?

Well, both of those things are fairly likely at some point and if you're not careful then that could have a serious impact on your business if you are relying on those for all of your enquiries.

Who is to even say that Facebook will remain the number one place that people hang out in the future? Sure, it is right now but things can change. And in the online world they change pretty fast.

From 2004 to 2010 MySpace was the number one ranked social media website in the world and in 2006 it overtook Google as the number one most visited website in the United States.

Overtook Google. You know, the search engine. Yes, that actually happened.

Now I don't know if you even remember MySpace or not but they've since changed hands a number of times, had a number of relaunches and facelifts but are now only the 4,153rd most popular website in terms of traffic. That's a significant fall from grace, I'm sure you'll agree.

What would have happened if you'd had a business built solely off the back of promotions on MySpace? I am sure lots of music businesses did and if they didn't move quick and change their strategies up then they're probably more surviving than thriving right now. If they're even that lucky.

Of course you've been long advised not to put all of your proverbial eggs into one basket and this is certainly the case here.

Sadly it's also a very common problem. Here's what often happens; you open up and start off with the basics. Maybe even what you see others doing (more on that in a moment). You have some mild success with that and continue doing more and more of it. You never get around to trying anything new because 'what you're doing works' or 'that would never work in your business'. Sound at all familiar?

Look, I'm going to level with you right now. If you rely on any fewer than ten different forms of getting new clients in to your business and getting existing clients back then you need to address that. Like, now.

Our beauty business actively does at least twenty-six of the above list and there are plenty more which we're planning for the future too!

You can do that for your business too, and I'm going to show you a system which I use and that you can copy. It's simple to implement and it doesn't even have to cost you any money. Sound good?

Now before I explain what this system is, there is something else you need to grasp. You need to track your marketing efforts.

If the previous chapter didn't hammer that point home enough, I'm going to mention it again here. After all, repetition is the mother of all learning.

This concept is especially important for the system I'm about to share with you. It won't work if you're guessing about whether your marketing works or not (which, by the way, there is no shame in — most people do guess — just accept that now's the time you're going to address that once and for good).

Okay, so now that you've committed to actually tracking all of your marketing then I think you're ready to hear all about the system.

It's deliciously simple and easy to follow.

Here goes…

actions for the band to commence the drum roll

1. Start by picking one of the marketing pillars from the list (or one of your own if you prefer). If you're on a very tight budget then feel free to start with one of the free ones. There are plenty of those.

2. Commit to trialling your new marketing pillar for one month.
3. At the end of the month work out how much profit that marketing pillar has generated for you. Not income, bottom line profit.
4. Calculate how much the campaign has cost you. Remember to include your time costs, printing costs, design costs and any other costs you incurred to get the campaign moving.
5. Subtract the total costs incurred from the first profit figure. Did you still make a profit or did you barely break even?
6. If it was profitable then run it again the next month. In fact, continue to do so every month for as long as it brings you in a profit. If it wasn't profitable then either bin the idea or tweak it to see if you can get a better return. This is important as a terribly designed leaflet might generate you zero profit but that doesn't mean leaflet drops as a whole might never work.
7. In month two you continue with the first pillar (if successful) and you start another one.
8. Run both for the month as explained before.
9. Determine at month end whether this new pillar has been a success or not.
10. Repeat the entire process for as long as you want to grow your business!

The system is really very simple indeed.

But please don't underestimate the power of it. This methodical testing removes the guesswork involved in so much marketing.

John Wanamaker famously said, "*Half the money I spend on advertising is wasted; the trouble is I don't know which half.*" Wanamaker died in 1893 and marketing has come rather a long way since. At least, the tracking and testing of it has.

Today there is little to no excuse for it as there are so many ways for you to determine without fail whether or not your marketing works. I'll even go as far as to say that if you don't think you can accurately test a certain marketing pillar then first try one you can instead.

After doing this for a year or so you might have six to eight new marketing pillars for your business which you know are working for you. At the same time you'll have also discarded another six or so which you know aren't for you. That's some mighty powerful marketing information right there in your pocket.

One final word of warning for this chapter.

When many businesses start up - or are on the look out for new customers — they copy what their competition are doing. So if they see their main competitors are doing Facebook adverts then they start running them too, assuming that if it works for one then it must work for another.

Be very careful if this is you.

Firstly, you don't know if your competitors are actually tracking their own marketing efforts. In fact, there is every chance that they aren't. Very few businesses indeed do this properly.

Secondly, are they even worth imitating? Seriously! The number of people who copy what their competition do is staggering; but in all seriousness do you really want to be like them?

Now of course they might be the number business in the whole country, profiting millions per year and delighting each and every client who passes through their door.

Or they might be one week from closure, selling treatments that make no profit, have unhappy and disloyal staff and have an owner who works 100 hours per week just to cover the rent.

Yes, these are extremes, but do you *really* know how well a competitor is doing behind the scenes?

Success leaves tracks. But then, so does failure. Be careful whose you are following.

4. All Customers Are Created Equal

I once had a sales manager who told me, "a client, is a client, is a client."

Aside from being grammatically poor, what this translated to was that all clients are worth the same as each other. Or, to put it another way, all clients are each other's equal.

Therefore it stands to reason that all clients should be treated the same. They should pay the same prices as one another, they should receive the same service as one another and they should each qualify for the same promotions.

Right? Or wrong? Do you currently treat all of your clients the same way?

You probably do. Most businesses treat all their clients in the exact same way. I'm certainly treated the same way as everyone else when I go to the supermarket, for example. I shop in a sea of equals.

My local paper shop treat me the same as everyone else, too. Although to be fair they do let me carry the dog in when it's officially no dogs allowed. Oh, and they put a newspaper aside for my Dad each day too. But other than that, it's all the same.

Same with my bank, too. Treated like another number. Except they did upgrade me to a 'Premier Account' recently. That was cool. The phone gets answered much quicker. And I get some free insurance and other stuff. And a better interest rate if I borrow money. So, yeah, not quite the same now I think about it...

So maybe everyone *doesn't* treat me the same, after all?

Let's take the example of my bank for a moment.

Now, I'm a good customer for my bank. Bizarrely I did work experience in my local branch when I was 15 or 16 and on the last day they thoughtfully opened an account for me. I still have that exact same account to this very day.

Plus over that time period I'd estimate that I've probably had a couple of credit cards, at least three car loans, two mortgages, various savings accounts, a couple of ISAs, a TESSA (ask your parents) and enough currency conversions to fund a military coup.

Additionally, I've never as much been late with one repayment to them. That makes me a pretty good customer in their eyes. They make money from me, have some of my money to invest on my behalf (and make even more from) plus they know I'll pay them back when I say I will.

Now compare that banking profile with that of someone with a less desirable repayment record. They might be constantly in their overdraft, making late repayments on loans which require collections departments to make endless phone calls and arrangements to repay, their cards are constantly declined and they take up lots of staff time trying to sort everything out for them.

Now, honestly, do you think we're equals as clients *in the bank's eyes?* Are we both worth the same to the bank as clients? Or would the bank rather have two of me if they could?

Well quite simply they'd rather have a thousand of me if they could. Why wouldn't they? They make more money from having me as a client *and* I cause them no grief whatsoever.

And that's exactly why they gave me a 'Premier Account' recently. They clearly want to hang onto me as a client for another twenty-five years.

So let's bring this back to your business.

Based on my banking tale, do you now think that your customers are equal? Do you truly believe that you should be treating these two clients in the same way?

A. Mrs Goggins. Has been a client since you started. A friend of your Mum's and she comes in like clockwork every Friday morning. Always brings a different friend with her and is forever spreading the good word of your business. She always buys products to take home with her and is always so sweet, thoughtful and caring toward you and all of your staff. Sometimes she even brings a box of cookies for all the girls to share!

B. Mrs Jones. First introduced to your business as a result of a Groupon experiment you once conducted. Paid a hugely reduced price and now asks for that same discount every time she visits. Always has bad things to say about everyone and really brings the whole place down when she comes in. Will say that she's happy and then go home and leave an unfair review on Facebook in the hope of future reduced treatments. Never buys any products when offered. Has poor personal hygiene.

So, what do you think? Should you be welcoming Mrs Goggins and Mrs Jones with equally open arms into your business? Of course not!

You see what I'm getting at here is that not all of your clients are created equally. Not by a long shot. Some are wonderful and should be recognised as such. Some are a terrible fit and should be fired.

That last sentence was not a misprint and I'll come on to that in moment, once I've let the idea sink in a little.

Now, have you ever heard of Vilfredo Pareto? If you're big on your seventeenth century Italian economists then he'll be a poster boy for you, however I'll forgive you if that's not your cup of tea.

Pareto is famous for his principle which shares his name, *the Pareto Principle*, which states that for many events roughly 80% of effects come from 20% of the causes.

You may have otherwise heard of this as the 80/20 rule. It's relevance here is that you'll find, with a predictable certainty, that 80% of your income as a business will come from 20% of your clients.

Let's explore that idea further. Let's say you have 100 clients. Some of them come every week and have lots of treatments, some of them have only ever been to see you once. If you totalled up everything each one had ever spent with you then you'll find that roughly 80% of all of that income you've received has come from just 20 of the 100 clients.

The maths isn't the important bit here. The takeaway is that you need to find the 20% in your business and treat them like freaking royalty!

They are the ones whom your business is really built on. They are the ones who take the upsells, come to your pop-up events, share your posts on social media, buy products from you and bring in friends when they come in for treatments.

You should know who these people are in your business and if you don't then there is a piece of homework for you. Go and identify them, now.

So what are you going to do with these 'top 20%' now?

Well, to begin with you'll want to assess every way in which you can make them feel even more special than you already do. Oh, and importantly, more special than everyone else.

Now if you're thinking at this point, *"I want to make all my customers feel special"*, then that's very admirable — however for the sake of your future you want to come up with some ways that these people can be super-duper-special-with-glitter-on-top.

Do you offer a VIP scheme of any description? Well maybe you should, and all of these people should be invited to join it. For free.

So this could mean preferential *anything*, depending on your business. For example free mini treatments, upgrades, posh coffees, biscuits, free parking, VIP nights, discounts on products, early access to new launches, dedicated VIP booking number, guaranteed senior staff member conducting treatments… whatever works for your business.

You might even want to get some little gold credit cards made up that they can slip into their purse. Make them feel special. Because then they'll keep coming back. More, and more, and more.

All of your staff should know who these clients are and they should all greet them by name and know their drinks order. If you've ever walked into a business and been greeted with something along the lines of, *"Morning Miss Green, your normal cappuccino today?"*, then you'll know how that makes you feel.

Like. A. Star. Make your clients feel like that.

Now this isn't about giving massive discounts. It's about making your very best customers *feel* like they are your best customers. It's about the experience and how you're treating them whilst they are with you.

Why? Well first of all, if you're just offering a discount then someone else can always offer a larger one. That's not a game you want to be competing in. Also, we don't remember discounts for very long. Yes, there is a quick thrill at the time of the discount but we don't walk around for the rest of the day beaming about it and telling everyone we speak to.

When we get a truly remarkable and personal experience from a business however, then we certainly do remember that all day. In fact, we'll remember it for a long time after the event and will do doubt tell anyone who wants to listen. Part of the reason we'll remember it is because very few people do it. And that almost certainly includes your competitors.

Once you're aware of it, you'll notice the 80/20 rule appearing all over the place.

20% of your activities will produce 80% of your results. 80% of your product sales will come from 20% of your sales people.

Or how about this one;

80% of your problems will be created by 20% of your customers.

So I touched on this earlier and it's so true. If I asked you to name your five *worst* customers, could you? The ones whose name you fear seeing in your diary. The ones where staff members flee when they walk through the door. The ones who you dread receiving an email from after they've been in with you.

You know the ones. Every business has them. It's natural to. Just like having some best customers, you've some worse ones too. And the problem is that this handful of 'difficult' clients are going to be responsible for far more than their fair share of problems.

It's time to sack them. Yup, I'm suggesting you fire your worst customers. The ones who are always late. Or always cancel at the last minute. Or don't respect your staff, your time and your business.

You don't have to tolerate customers like those. Honestly, you don't.

Now I fully realise that you may be thinking I've gone mad (I've not, I promise). You may think it's in some way illegal (nope), immoral (no) or unfair (it's unfair on you and your team if anything, to have to keep dealing with these awful people).

Just like you want to find your best customers and treat them like superstars, you also want to find your worst customers and show them the door.

Wouldn't you rather spend your time dealing with the nice ones? The ones who refer you more business and brighten up your day? Well do it then! You're the boss and you get to decide who you do business with and who you don't.

You'll want to discuss this with the clients first, and if there are certain elements of their behaviour which you want them to change then simply tell them! Explain that if they are late then their treatment times will be effected and that they'll still be charged if they fail to give you enough notice when they cancel an appointment.

If they continue to repeat offend then it's time to stop offering your services to them. Explain to them that you've realised that perhaps you aren't the best business to look after them and their needs moving forward. You've tried but seem unable to make them happy and whilst you'll be sorry to see them go you think they might be happier at a different salon.

Probably best to conduct this over the telephone and when they aren't in your premises. Now I know that this isn't easy. There are lots of times that business isn't.

However by doing this you're going to make your work life happier in the long run. Yes, you run the risk of them slagging you off afterward. So be it. Focus on the damage they are doing to your business, to your staff, to your other clients, maybe even on your own sanity. Cut the cord.

5. The Customer Is Always Right

Hot on the heels of encouraging you to sack some of your clients, you've probably already worked out how I feel about whether or not the customer is *always* right. (Or even occasionally right, in some cases).

Now before I launch myself fully into this topic, I want to make something very clear. I completely and whole-heartedly agree with the idea of offering outstanding client satisfaction. In fact, I want to go a step further than that. I don't really want my clients being satisfied. I want them to be delighted. Ecstatic, even. Walking away wondering why all experiences can't be like the one they've just had.

I will go the extra mile for my clients. I want them to love me and my business and I'd very much like it if they were clients for life. Heck, I'd love it if they introduced me to their friends, too!

But (and this is a great big, unapologetically in-your-face kind of but), that doesn't mean they are always right. Furthermore, I genuinely believe that adopting this attitude of the customer always being right is actually *harming* your business. Yup, for reals.

Before I explain my reasons for this, let's fleetingly dive back into the proverbial history books to get a little understanding about how this term became so ingrained in our business culture.

It's believed that Harry Gordon Selfridge — the founder of the high-end department stores which bare his name — first coined the phrase, sometime around 1909.

It's important to note at this point that retail in 1909 was a little different to how it is today. There were no shopping precincts or arcades. Indeed, shopping was only due to a necessity at that time and the idea of shopping for pleasure would have been deemed absurd.

How times have changed! Business in the twentieth century was governed by the overriding principle of *caveat emptor*, a Latin phrase meaning, "let the buyer beware".

This means that the onus was on the customer to make sure that they were happy with everything prior to purchase, and not afterward, and to assume that the seller knows more about the goods than they do.

Back in 1909 consumer laws didn't exist and buyers had nothing like the protection they are afforded now. Now customers are protected by the Sale of Goods Act 1979 and the Consumer Rights Act 2015. There was nothing of such like in 1909. They didn't even have social media to whoop, moan, complain and holler all over!

This meant of course that Harry Selfridge promoting the consumer as a champion was something out of the ordinary. Indeed, no doubt this was a form of competitive advantage for his business as it was something others weren't doing.

Of course, that's not the case now. There are statutory rights as mentioned above which means the law protects customers against wrong doing, faulty goods, unfair purchase terms and more.

Customer service as a source of competitive advantage is harder to achieve now purely because customers expect great service wherever they go. The power shift has long taken place already!

This is partly why I believe that the idea of granting further, almost absolute, power to the customer isn't required now and actually is an unhelpful concept which might in turn hurt your business.

Let's look at some more reasons why this concept is now outdated, in a more practical manner. To begin with, I believe that the customer already has plenty of protection. The law is on their side and any business which I've ever been involved with is always going to offer good, and fair, customer service.

However by taking this a step further and suggesting that each and every customer is *always* right, I believe, offers an unfair advantage to your worst customers.

I mean, they could now demand anything they liked, right?

Huge discounts, free treatments, speaking to your staff however they please, wandering in late for appointments, expecting preferential treatment when they visit, priority bookings… *anything*.

Because, after all, they're always right. And by that rationale you've got to at least entertain, if not comply, with any suggestions or demands they make. Now, of course, that's sheer lunacy.

Not least because you know full well that those customers who try and take advantage of this are your most demanding ones! (The ones I encouraged you to sack in the last chapter, remember? Yup, them again!).

As a business, we all have limited resources. Time, staff, money and even energy. Dealing with these clients who are seemingly never happy with your attempts to satisfy their needs will quickly deplete all of these resources.

Oh, and your sanity, morale and faith in the human race too. They'll also be depleted very quickly indeed. Don't waste your time and efforts in trying to constantly bend over backwards to appease a small number of awkward and demanding clients. Sack them, and focus your time on all of those other, much happier, customers instead.

Every business of any size will have its fair share of awkward, rude or snappy customers. The law of averages states we'll all have some of those. However by supporting these customers and backing them when they are upset about something will often mean that you're taking their side against someone a lot more important to you. Your staff.

Think about it for a moment.

When a customer moans about a situation (fairly or otherwise) and you back them against your staff, doing all you can to make them happy again, you're actually putting them ahead of your employees. That is not going to be good for staff morale. In fact, it's going to be disastrous.

The entire concept of the customer being right means that someone else is wrong. Probably the person who is dealing with them. This immediately pits one against the other, and with one having a clear advantage.

With time this is sure to demoralise your troops, potentially result in bitterness aimed toward you as a business owner and moreover it emphasises that as a business you favour customers ahead of employees.

Wouldn't it be much better if you had the faith in your employees to deal with these situations instead? As opposed to blindly favouring the client? I think so.

Richard Branson takes a wonderfully opposing standpoint to this entire idea. The Virgin Group founder — and multi-billionaire no less — believes that employees should always be backed and always come first.

He says, "If you look after your staff well, they will look after your customers". I like this idea. Let's take it a little bit further.

Let's first think about what might happen when the company and management consistently side with customers ahead of employees. Hal Rosenbluth, author of *Put The Customer Second - Put Your People First And Watch'em Kick Butt,* argues that it sends a clear message that;

- employees are not valued
- treating employees fairly is not important
- employees have no right to respect from customers
- employees have to put up with everything from customers

Not wonderful messages to send to your staff!

Conversely, if you put your staff first then they'll be much happier at work. Happy employees will naturally give far superior service in the first place because;

- they care more about other people, including customers
- they have more energy
- they are happy, meaning they are more fun to talk to and interact with
- they are more motivated

Which would you prefer in your business?

To finally put an exclamation point on this topic, it stands to reason that sometimes people are wrong.

I'm wrong sometimes, you are, everyone is. The customer can't possibly be right all the time!

Remember also that those who are often disgruntled and wish to take advantage of this standpoint are often clients who you will never satisfy. Some people will simply never be happy. You don't need them in your business.

6. People Always Want The Cheapest Deals

One of the biggest fears shared with me by my coaching clients is that of new competition springing up overnight.

You go to bed one night and then the next thing you know there are two new salons or nail bars just yards from your business.

And - worst of all - they're cheaper than you.

Dun-dun-dunnnnnnnn!

The fear of course comes when you believe that you'll then instantly lose all of your best clients or worry that you'll have to drop your prices to compete with your new neighbours.

Because customers always want the cheapest deals they can get. Don't they?

That's the common conception. Or rather, misconception. The fact of the matter is that not all customers want the cheapest treatments, products or services that they can get.

Indeed, studies have shown only around 20% of consumers rank price as the single most important factor when making a purchase. Naturally, this will vary from industry to industry, but you can use it as a yardstick for now.

Just think about it for a minute. Do you always buy the cheapest food you can? Value beans on economy bread for dinner again, is it?

How about clothes? Is everyone walking around in second half castoffs from the charity shop?

Perhaps everyone wants the cheapest transport they can get. So why aren't they all driving beaten up 1985 Ford Fiestas? Or taking the bus instead? Or just walking?!

The truth is that price isn't the only consideration when people are making a buying decision.

It's a consideration — and for some people a more important consideration than others — but there is more to it than simply the number of hard earned pounds being handed over. Especially in our industry. Maybe not if you're in a commoditised industry of some sort — such as if you sell nuts and bolts or computer paper. For us, in the experience industry, price is not the key factor driving the decision for the majority of your clients.

Now here's a key point and I really don't want you to miss this.

Some people do want the cheapest they can get of everything. Some people do eat beans on toast every day, do get their clothes from charity shops and do take the bus everywhere.

You do not want those people as your clients.

Let them go to the new salon up the road. Heck, you can even give them a lift there in your car if you like! (They don't have one, remember?)

Let them be a headache for someone else as that is what they'll become. These type of clients who are so focussed on price will be the same clients who expect you to go the extra mile for them without reward. They'll expect freebies. They'll moan at your staff. They'll leave mediocre reviews.

They may refer you some people. Sadly these people are likely to be their friends and will most probably share their mindset. Then after all of that, they'll not even be loyal. As soon as there is another cheaper option elsewhere, they'll be off.

So the next time a 'cheap as chips' pop-up salon arrives overnight on your doorstep don't be sad. Instead be delighted that they're about to take your most awkward clients off your hands and allow you to concentrate on serving your more deserving ones.

Whilst that last comment was a little tongue-in-cheek, I'm serious about the sentiment. You shouldn't be aiming your business at the lower end of the market. Aim high as that's where the clients who will value you and your expertise are, those who will gladly pay you what you ask and who will happily bring along more friends with them too.

They can probably also afford to come and see you more regularly and even buy the products you recommend to them. Doesn't that sound better?

In additional good news, most people aim at the middle or the lower end of the market so there's generally less competition the higher you set your sights.

So now the myth of everyone wanting the cheapest they can get has been busted, what are people basing their buying decisions on, and how can you take advantage?

Well, quite simply, there are lots and lots of different factors but here are some that you might want to consider.

<u>Reviews</u>

Reviews matter. A lot. People read them and, by and large, people trust them.

How are the testimonials, case studies and reviews on your website looking?

closes eyes and preys that you have some

How about your Google reviews? If you don't have any, then consider this to be your wake up call. You need them, now.

You should consider collecting your reviews in a number of different ways. To begin with you should have some you've collected yourself. These may be more in the form of client testimonials or case studies than reviews, per se, but they are still important.

As you've collected these yourself people will be naturally more suspicious of them. Therefore consider video reviews as, quite frankly, people will think you'll have been less likely to have made these up.

Reviews and testimonials on your own website which are text only (and even worse, without even a picture) scream out, "I've been made up, disregard me!" Get some recorded on video instead; ideally with the client clearly explaining what their problem was, how they felt before and now how they feel that you've solved it for them.

Reviews are seen as far more authoritative (and less likely works of fiction) when they are hosted on a trusted third-party website.

You should actively be encouraging all of your clients to review you on Google (not least because it will massively help your Google search rankings), perhaps TripAdvisor (for those clients without Gmail accounts) and maybe even a known industry site such as SalonSpy.

You really cannot receive too many reviews, so you should be requesting them from all of your clients, all of the time. In an ideal situation when someone is looking you up then they should be completely overwhelmed by the number of reviews and have any shadow of doubt removed.

Oh, and don't worry about the occasional negative review. Every business gets them. It's natural. Your potential new clients will allow you a few as they realise that you can't possibly please everyone every time. In actual fact the occasional negative review can be seen in a positive light; it makes all the others look even more legitimate.

People Are Sheep

Despite the increased number of people you see walking the streets with face tattoos, tunnel earrings and bright blue hair, as a society we are for the most part followers.

We like to see what others are doing and in an ideal world we'd like to do the same, please. Are you more likely to go into the empty pub, or the crowded one?

Well, studies show the more crowded one attracts us more. The idea that you might be missing out on something wonderful is too much pressure for most people. And after all there must be a good reason why nobody is in the empty one, right?

Yes, we are sheep at heart. One person does something and everyone else follows them.

However you can of course work this to your advantage too. Many of our preferences are learned and formed by social behaviour, norms and expectations. Straying too far from these norms might just hurt your business.

Does everyone seemingly have magazines in their waiting area? Coffee and biscuits for each guest? A friendly smile upon entry?

If so, then you'd better be doing it too. People will expect it, and won't like it should they not receive it. Regardless of how 'cutting edge' you're trying to be by doing it your own way.

Furthermore, people will also follow the crowds on social media. You can bet that potential new customers will be looking you up on social media. Probably on multiple networks. I read recently an article suggesting that people are more likely to turn to your social media accounts even before your website when researching your business for the first time.

Has your account been updated recently with some interesting, educational or entertaining posts? Are all of the details regarding opening hours and parking up to date? Do you have more than 500 fans?

If not then you can be sure that this is hurting you. People will be checking on you and then making a snap decision about whether or like to give you a try. Make that decision as easy as possible for them.

Keep It Simple, Stupid

Sometimes in business we just make it unnecessarily difficult. Your aim is to make it as easy as possible for someone to do business with you.

There is nothing more annoying than when businesses put unnecessary blocks in place to prevent you buying from them. The easier you make it, the more money you'll receive. It's as simple as that!

Only want to accept cash? That's a barrier.

Only have parking which people have to pay for? That's a barrier.

Have a confusing menu which is difficult to read or understand? That's another barrier.

Doorway and entrance looking weathered and uninviting? Yup, a barrier.

You get the picture. Think about the customer experience and journey and make it easy for them to give you money! Ask your existing clients what you could improve upon and make the changes. Business doesn't have to be difficult but lots of times we overcomplicate things when we don't need to.

Remember the acronym K.I.S.S. and keep it simple, stupid!

Convenience

Another factor in our time-poor lives is convenience. Everybody is forever rushing from place to place in today's society and has less and less time to spend on themselves.

This can, of course, be an issue for our industry.

Is it convenient for people to do business with you? Are you open the hours when they need you? Are you located where they can easily access you? Is there ample parking or are you on a major public transport route? Is it easy to find you or are you nestled away somewhere? Will my sat nav take me directly to your door?

There is a good reason why the smaller Tesco Express stores are more expensive than their supermarket counterparts. You're paying for the convenience of their location and how simple it is to pop in and collect that loaf of bread you'd forgotten. People will happily pay the premium for convenience, and it's important in a society which is getting lazier and lazier.

Familiarity

It's far easier to get clients returning to you once they've been wowed by you once. The tricky thing is getting them through your door for the first time.

However just because they've not been to see you doesn't mean that these potential new clients don't know who you are. I've never been into an Aston Martin dealership but I sure am familiar with the brand!

Market yourself more. Get your name out there across many different advertising platforms. Remember not to rely on too few marketing pillars.

And this is only part of the story. People will also consider other factors too, such as;

- Customer experience
- Staff credentials
- Brand reputation
- Quality and choice of treatments offered
- Safety
- Ambience
- Value (not the same as price)
- Payment options
- Speed of delivery or response

Of course for each person the most important element will change. This is why you must understand all of these different reasons for buying and consider them within your business. People by and large will consider a variety of these reasons and make a decision on balance.

Perhaps now you appreciate that the price isn't the only factor which drives decision making!

Funnily enough, whilst there are an estimated 20% of the market who are always looking for the least expensive solution to their problems, they have a direct opposite too.

Another estimated 20% of the market who are always looking for the *most* expensive solution to their problems. These people take pride in boasting about how much they paid for something. It helps them to justify to themselves how important they are. But irrespective of how you feel toward that idea, these people are out there, they exist and they make great clients!

Please don't think either that these people are in any way different to you and I. There are many times when I'll buy the most expensive items or versions on the menu. I don't want poor tasting coffee. I don't want the cheapest glass of wine. I certainly don't want the cheapest food.

That doesn't make me stuck up, toffee-nosed or even wealthy. I am just someone who really likes those things and therefore would much rather have the best version of them (or at the very least, not the cheapest)! It will be the same for your clients.

So maybe you should flip your thinking on its head here. As opposed to worrying about whether your prices are low enough, consider if they are high enough! Add some exclusive or VIP versions of some of your existing treatments and products. Longer treatments, more extras, bigger bundles. Make sure you're also catering for those clients who want to spend much, much more with you. Are you giving your best clients the chance to spend a small fortune with you, should they want to?

If you add these more expensive items to your menu not only will they make everything else look less expensive but some people will buy them, I guarantee it. But if they don't know about it then they can't. It's your job to let them know.

One final word of warning for this chapter.

Please, don't get into a price war. There are no winners in any war, this type included. Your pricing must be calculated in a methodical way at all times, with a careful analysis of your costs and with valuing your time as a skilled and qualified professional.

Please do not under any circumstances start randomly slashing your prices because you've seen someone else do it. You do not know their costs. You do not know their income expectations. You do not have to do the same.

Are you thinking enough about those who want to come and spend more money with you or are you too busy worrying about how you can reduce your prices to accommodate those with smaller purses?

Sounds silly that, doesn't it?

Yet lots of business owners do just that. Don't be one of them.

7. The Only Way To Grow Your Business Is To Get More Customers

Sometime we over complicate business when it needn't be that difficult.

One of the simplest ways to double your business is simply to charge twice as much for your treatments. Now that may sound rather blasé and over simplified —however mathematically it's accurate.

Naturally, that's not to say you can just charge twice as much as you currently do *for the same thing* and hope to retain your entire client base. However if you can find a way to increase the amount of money your clients spend with you each time they are in your presence then you'll get to where you want to go much quicker than relying on constantly attracting new clients (which is what the majority of business owners focus on).

As Jay Abraham famously observed there are three — and only three — ways to grow your business.

1. Increase the number of clients you serve
2. Increase the frequency of purchase
3. Increase the average client spend

That's it!

They are the only ways in which you can grow as everything falls into one of those three categories.

One of the common pitfalls for many business owners in any industry is that they all concentrate on number one; increasing the number of clients they serve. This is an oversight for a number of reasons.

First and foremost continually finding new clients is both exhausting and expensive. In fact, attracting new clients is both the most challenging and most costly way of the three. Yet time and time again it's where the focus lies.

Most business owners would be better advised (plus probably saner and with more money left in their pockets) to focus on the other two first.

Think about it for a minute.

Do you think it would be easier to convince someone who knows of you and your expertise already to come back and see you again for another treatment — or convince someone who has never heard of you to try you out for the first time?

Now the answer to that question I am hoping should be fairly obvious but just in case let's consider an example.

Let's say you're out for some drinks with a group of friends and you decide to grab something to eat to soak up some of the wine you've been consuming. (Crazy scenario, I know, but try and imagine that!)

You've two options; one is *Nando's* and the other a new Portuguese chicken-based restaurant called *Dando's* (who can probably expect a letter from Nando's legal team in the near future, for what it's worth).

Everyone in the group has heard of Nando's and over half have eaten there before. Everyone is familiar with who they are, what they do and most have enjoyed their food previously.

Nobody has ever tried Dando's as it's new to town. Which do you think the group are more likely to settle on?

All else being equal, I'd argue it's safe to say that Nando's is likely to win this little contest. As human beings most people want certainty. Something they already know and enjoy is likely to win over the unknown.

Therefore it'll be the same for you and your clients. Getting your existing clients back through your door is always going to be much easier (and less expensive) than finding new ones.

Now, do you think that it's easier to again go out and find new clients or would it be easier to encourage your existing clients to spend more money when they are with you?

Let's look at another example.

I'm going to assume here you're familiar with the concept of the hamburger chain *McDonald's* and I'm going to go a step further and assume you've eaten in one too. If you order a Big Mac from the menu, what's the next question you're asked by the server? Wherever you are in the world, regardless of which of the 36,909 restaurants you've chosen, the reply will be, "Would you like fries with that?"

I have no idea of the percentage of people who take up this generous and thoughtful offer but I'm convinced it makes up a substantial chunk of their grease-laden profits.

You see McDonald's know that the very best time to sell something to anyone is immediately after you've sold them something else.

You've probably noticed many other retailers — both online and offline — catching on and doing the same. And so they should, as it's a smart thing to do. It's a great way to bump up the average client spend in a way which is not intrusive, is widely accepted by the client and moreover is hugely profitable for the company.

So to bring this full circle, there are more ways to grow your business than just constantly focussing on getting more bodies through your door. And more to the point, there are simpler and more cost effective ways too.

Now this isn't to say don't try to attract new clients, but it is to say don't solely focus your efforts on this. There are lower hanging fruits to harvest and you should start with those.

So whilst I'm certainly not advocating blindly doubling your prices I do believe that you must look at practical ways that you can increase your client's average spend with you.

The reason why this is so powerful is two-fold in my opinion.

Firstly, in many instances the client has already committed to making a purchase with you mentally and emotionally. The actual pounds and pence are no longer going to be influencing the decision as much as you might believe.

Secondly, I believe that a higher value sale is no harder to close than a lower one. Yes, I'm saying that it's just as easy to make a £100 sale as it is a £10 one. Or even a £10,000 sale over a £10 one. And I would know, as I've done both many, many times.

You see most of the time the client has already made the decision to commit to a purchase long before the price has even been discussed. In their mind they are already enjoying the treatment, service or product. Assuming they like and trust you then there is no reason why the sale won't happen.

Providing that the client is, in their mind, receiving enough value for the price you are asking then the sale will occur. At any price.

So therefore when we are looking at ways in which we can increase the overall client spend what we must really focus on is providing even greater value for the client. Ideally so much of it that they just can't say no!

Before we look at some specific strategies which you can implement in your own business, I think it's really important to flush out a couple of potential demons in your mind which may prevent you from getting the higher ticket sales. Or, in many cases, even asking for those sales!

One of the cardinal mistakes which any sales person can ever make is confusing what *they* can afford with what their client can. If you're promoting a high end cosmetic treatment for over £1,000 and you're thinking, "I would never pay that much for a treatment", then you need to be careful!

Those subconscious thoughts will come across and you'll end up not selling many of these treatments at all — either you'll sabotage the sale yourself or will inadvertently put the client off. All whilst blaming the treatment or the fact that "nobody around here could afford that"!

Just because you can't or wouldn't pay a given price for something doesn't mean that nobody else will. Remember, you are not your client.

The second sales demon is located right in between your ears. For many less successful salespeople there is a little voice in their head who says things to them such as;

"This person doesn't look like they could afford the higher priced treatment, offer them the lower one", or...

"I don't have a good feeling about this one", or...

"I've already sold one today so that's good. It doesn't matter if I don't sell any more".

They are already talking themselves out of the sale before they've even opened their mouth!

Much of selling comes down to confidence. You must believe in yourself and your ability. You must believe in what you're selling and that it can genuinely benefit your client. You must believe that you're going to get the sale when you ask for it.

And most importantly you must ask for the sale, every time.

I understand totally that many, many people in our industry don't like sales. They see it as the dirty part of the industry. The part they'd rather not do and if the boss isn't watching then there's every chance they'll do anything to avoid the situation altogether.

Much of this comes down to a lack of two things; training and confidence. And of course, when the business owner lacks the confidence to sell too then what sort of an example is that going to set?

It is a problem though, because as stated at the top of the chapter this is one of the easiest ways to grow your business - as well as have your staff grow your business, too. I'm not just talking about selling products here, I'm talking about upselling treatments and packages too.

What will help is making them so irresistible to your clients that much of the selling is done for you already. Let's look at some ways you can do that now.

Packages and VIP Offers

One of the simplest ways to increase the average client spend is simply by offering a VIP or luxury version of the treatments which you already offer. Almost every treatment can be made into a luxury version, either by extending the treatment time or by including some extras to make it into a mini-package.

The keys here are that firstly you want to add enough additional value for the client that they are tempted to go for the more expensive option. Making sure, of course, that you've done your sums before you've priced the packages up.

Secondly, everyone must ask if the client wants the luxury version *every* time. It can be casually asked, and the client really won't mind, but you'll be amazed by the number of clients who will gladly say yes - if you just ask them. Seriously, try it.

Menu Design

The design and layout of restaurant menus is big business. Conversely most treatment menus are thrown together or left in the hands of a graphic designer. These can be costly mistakes and a little more thought could turn into lots more money in your till.

The psychology of pricing and sales is something which you shouldn't overlook. Have you been to a city centre gastropub recently? You may have noticed that the way they write the prices has changed.

It was once £11.50

Then it became £11.5

Now it's often just expressed simply as 11.5

Same price, different psychology. Why? Well because some boffins have discovered that simply by removing the pound symbol we subconsciously disassociate the financial element of the decision.

We're choosing the dish we want more than the price we want to pay. Removing the zero makes it appear even less like a monetary amount.

The result of this? The studies show that average spend goes up. How easy would this be to implement in your business?

The psychology doesn't stop there, either. There are plenty of other examples we can lean on which can also help in bumping up our profitability.

Now for this to work you need to know which treatments you would rather sell. Are there some on your menu which are more profitable than others? (And in case you're unsure, there absolutely are, by the way, and it's your job to know which they are!)

Are you giving these treatments the same credence on your menu as all the others? If so, why?

You'll find on restaurant menus some items are in a larger font. Or a bold typeface. Or perhaps they have a little box around them to highlight them. These are known in the design industry as 'eye magnets' and are there to do exactly as the name implies.

Studies also show that many people scan menus — lingering the longest on the first and last items listed. Make these the ones you want to sell.

Are your menu descriptions enticing enough? Or are you using the same standard stock descriptions that your clients have read hundreds of times before in all manner of other businesses? Do not underestimate the persuasive power of the words you use on your menu. Need some inspiration? Just go online and download the treatment menus of the very top spas and salons from across the world and pay attention to the language they use.

Menu designers have all sorts of little tips or tricks to draw your eye to certain dishes. The ones the restaurant owners want you to buy. It's a smart thing to do. Copy them.

<u>The Cinema Conundrum</u>

Popcorn is of course one of the highlights of any trip to the cinema. You might not have given the pricing strategy employed by the vendors much consideration up until this point, but make sure you pay attention on your next visit.

The pricing is usually very deliberate. Again you're duped into believing you have a free choice however the psychology behind it is calculated in such a way that the cinemas can predict with great accuracy what the majority of people will purchase. Naturally, it's been designed in their favour.

The coffee shops have cottoned on to this and employ similar tactics too.

Let's look at an example. Typically, there are three options for the your popcorn. There's the small, which, confusingly, is often called a medium. Let's say it's £3.

Then comes the medium (which is often called large) which comes in at, say, £5.50.

And then the large (called super, extra large, jumbo or whatever) which is £6.

Now, who in their right mind is going to purchase the medium for £5.50, when they can have the large for just 50p more?

Nobody is. And that's the point. It's a decoy. Those sneaky cinema owners put the medium in there just to make the large look as though it's better value than it really is.

Think about how your decision making might change should you only be offered the small or large. One at £3 and one at £6. The split might be fairly even in terms of how many people ordered the small against the large.

But when the medium is thrown into the mix then all of a sudden the large looks outrageously good value and becomes somewhat of a no-brainer. Exactly the same in Starbucks, Costa or wherever you like to buy your coffee from. They have done their maths and they know which they want you to purchase. Take a closer look next time you're grabbing a coffee or a film.

Moreover, how could you implement this in your own pricing strategies to encourage clients to spend more when they are with you? Do you offer any time-based treatments such as massage whereby you could copy this strategy?

Are you offering enough expensive treatments?

What is the most that someone could realistically spend with you in an afternoon? If it's less than £50 then the sad fact of the matter is that it's going to be difficult for you to achieve financial freedom at that rate.

Of course, that's not everyone's goal and that's fine, but given that you've purchased a book on marketing and business growth I'm going to assume that it's up there somewhere for you.

Now if you do value the freedom of choice which money brings you then you'll want to address this sooner rather than later.

There are some people who want to spend more money with you. In fact, much, much more money with you most likely if only you had some more expensive products or treatments to offer them.

Perhaps it's time to look at offering some more expensive treatments or services for your clients? There is such an array of machines which offer incredible results — you only have to take a stroll around one of the large industry exhibitions to find plenty of them.

What would the impact on your business be if you could start charging £100 per treatment as opposed to £25? Well, let's take a look at some numbers, shall we?

Now I'm well aware that not everyone loves mathematics so I am going to try and make this as simple and straightforward as I possibly can.

I am also going to bring this chapter full circle by referring once again to Jay Abraham's three ways to grow your business. In case they've slipped your memory already, they are:

1. Increase the number of clients you serve
2. Increase the frequency of purchase
3. Increase the average client spend

Let's use the following numbers by way of an example.
Let's assume you currently have 250 customers.
On average they visit you twice per year.
Each time they visit you they spend, on average, £25.

This would mean that your revenue for the year would be:

250 (number of customers) × 2 (number of visits) × £25 (average spend)

250 × 2 × 25 = £12,500 per year

Now let's take a look at what happens if you double the number of customers you have. Let's also remember that this is hardest and most expensive to achieve as these people don't know you.

That would then mean you have 500 customers. On average they visit you twice per year. Each time they visit you they spend, on average, £25.

This would mean that your revenue for the year would be:

500 (number of customers) × 2 (number of visits) × £25 (average spend)

$500 \times 2 \times 25 = £25,000$ per year

You've just doubled your business!

But of course, it's not quite that cut and dry. Not least because the costs to acquire all of those new customers are likely to be very high indeed. You may have doubled your revenue but certainly not your profits.

But what about if you manage to double your average client spend? Or manage to get people to come back and see you twice as often? Or both?!

Now, as discussed throughout this chapter (and indeed throughout the book) there are many, many things you can do to increase the regularity with which people visit you and there are also ways we've discussed to increase the client spend.

Doubling both would be no easy task, but for the purposes of this example, here's the impact that would have.

That would then mean you still have 250 customers. On average they visit you four times per year. Each time they visit you they spend, on average, £50.

This would mean that your revenue for the year would be:

250 (number of customers) × 4 (number of visits) × £50 (average spend)

$250 \times 4 \times 50 = £50,000$ per year

You've just quadrupled your business right there!

Now of course these numbers aren't necessarily realistic. But it's the mathematics which I wanted to illustrate to you.

You don't need to be concentrating solely on getting more customers in through your door all the time.

As you can hopefully now see there are simpler, and likely more profitable, ways to grow your business than just by trying to attract more clients. I'd thoroughly recommend looking at ways to increase your client average spend.

Perhaps through offering more expensive, results-driven treatments. Certainly by selling more products. Definitely by offering (and asking for) cross-sells and up-sells every time and by putting together new and more expensive packages for your guests.

Now of course not everyone is going to take your most expensive, all singing and all dancing, top-of-the-line, bonanza package. AKA 'the works'. But the point is that some people will if you put it on your menu, tell people about it and ask them to buy it.

I know that sounds ridiculously simple — and that's because it is. Think about how you can shake up your menu both in terms of what you're offering and how you're telling everyone about it.

8. You Need To Spend Thousands To Compete With 'Big Business'

Once upon a time it was incredibly difficult to start your own business. It was expensive. It was not always accepted socially. There were huge barriers to entry. Not so much now.

Businesses can be launched on a shoestring, practically overnight from someone's kitchen table. Start-up costs are at all all time low thanks to cost effective imports and subsidised rents.

Everyone wants to do it too — just look at the popularity of TV shows such as The Apprentice and Dragon's Den. Welcome to the age of the entrepreneur!

Many of these such businesses — maybe yours, too — are one woman (or man) bands. Solopreneurs as they've recently been dubbed.

And whilst these businesses may or may not employ any staff, they are almost exclusively local businesses. Serving a given, and usually fairly small, geographical area.

I am a big fan of local business and will always support it wherever and whenever I can. Being a small business owner myself I understand the struggles and frustrations, the early mornings and late nights, the highs and the lows of business ownership. You probably do too.

I always fear for the local newsagent who opens his shop at 6am every day (including weekends and bank holidays, thank you very much) when a new Tesco Express lands on his doorstep.

Or when Starbucks open another branch opposite a family ran coffee shop or cafe. Because the smaller businesses can't possibly compete with the larger ones, can they? And everyone would rather the wider choice and lower prices afforded by the bigger chains, wouldn't they? And for the smaller business to stand any chance of survival whatsoever they'd need to invest thousands in their marketing efforts, wouldn't they?

Yes, I know that's what you've been led to believe but let's consider challenging some of that, shall we?

I'm here with good news. Good news for me and for you. Good news for every small or local business in the land.

You *can* complete with the proverbial 'big boys'. And *not* everyone wants to use the larger multi-location stores and multinationals.

And you absolutely *can* market your business so that you're at capacity without spending thousands.

And yes, seeing as though we're here together I might as well tell you how you can do it too. This is probably an entire book in itself (hey, there's an idea for the follow up book!) but I want to demonstrate to you that no matter what the local market throws at you, you can fight back! Importantly, it needn't cost you the earth — or your sanity, either.

Now, a word of warning before I take you through this action plan. It's blindingly simple. There is nothing I'm going to cover here which you can't do. There are no fancy marketing strategies which require you to be a computer genius to apply. You will not need to hire a marketing company (or your tech-savvy 14 year old niece) to put any of this into place.

Yes, there are lots of exciting, quirky and geeky marketing strategies out there. I am a big advocate of many of them. But that's not the purpose of this chapter. I instead want to show you how you can compete with anything that comes at you without spending a fortune. The fancy stuff can come later.

The funny thing is that after you've finished this chapter you might wonder why everyone isn't doing it, given the simplicity involved.

Well, it's because most people are lazy. And the good news is that includes your competition. Just by taking action you'll be head and shoulders ahead of the pack, of that I promise you. If you take action on this plan, and then build on that with some of the other concepts and ideas in this book then you'll have a wonderful foundation for your business.

You've just got to do it.

So you'll remember from earlier in the book (I hope!) that we want to be focussing on identifying a small number of ideal clients. We're not going after the masses here, as it's expensive and there is no need.

What we want is a much smaller number of raving, loyal fans and your marketing efforts are going to be focussed solely on attracting those people to you.

Work out who those people are. Where they live, how old they are, which other businesses they like, what they do for a living, how many children they have — as much as you possibly can. Get a good mental picture of what they look like. Heck, you can even give them a name if you want. Everything you do is going to be in an attempt to draw these people in to you and keep them coming back time and time again.

When you have a clear idea of who it is you want to attract, your life as a marketer will become much easier. You can use the free downloadable dream client template to help you map this out.

Once you know this, you then need to get clear on the message you're going to be delivering to them.

What do you stand for as a business? What are you all about? What principles make you different to everyone else? What is it that you do better than the rest? You are much better off specialising in one certain area than appearing as a jack of all trades. After all, you know how the rest of that expression goes.

Perhaps you offer the best facials in Bath. Maybe you're the only true vegan salon in Ipswich. You could be the number one rated spa on TripAdvisor, have won more awards than anyone else or be the only supplier of a certain service or treatment. This is your USP (or unique selling proposition) and it should become the centre of your marketing. You'll want to shout about this at every given opportunity to make yourself stand out and attract your dream clients too.

Think about the positioning this gives you in the eyes of your clients.

I'd strongly recommend against having a USP of being the cheapest or the most affordable. That's a race to the bottom of the pile and you want to get as far away from that as possible.

Only after you've considered who you're trying to market to and what message you're conveying should you consider how you're going to get in front of these people.

Too often people make the mistake of thinking they need do a given type of marketing (for example, Facebook ads) and *then* they consider what they are going to say to whom.

This is the wrong way around. You must determine who you're looking to attract first, then what your message is and then finally figure out the best means of achieving it. Your marketing campaigns will be much more successful doing it this way around.

Back in chapter three I listed over 70 ways that you can get your message out there (although only aimed at your dream clients, remember). Now you can pick and choose whichever of these resonate with you the most, and I encourage you to try as many of them of possible over time, however I would start with the free ones.

Here's a wonderfully simple (and free) way to start. Now I'm going to assume you have a website with a blog on it. There's really no excuse in the twenty-first century to not have a website. You can have a simple but functional one built for you for next to nothing. Any web person will easily be able to add a blog for you, too.

Now you don't need to write hundreds of blog posts every month, but you do need to start adding some content centred around your message and the treatments and products you're trying to sell. People are out there actively searching for these on Google and you want to be the name which is showing up. Google will bring you an almost endless supply of clients, for free, if you're happy to play by their rules. Sounds to me like a game worth not only playing, but mastering.

Let's say your main treatment is microdermabrasion. You'll want to write a series of blogs all based around this. One stating all the benefits, one explaining why it's such a popular treatment, one stating that you offer it in your area. In an ideal world you want these to be based around the terms that people are searching for.

What would you type into Google if you wanted a microdermabrasion treatment, or were considering one?

Microdermabrasion in Bath

Bath microdermabrasion

Microdermabrasion Somerset

Best microdermabrasion Bath

Microdermabrasion near me

Salons that offer microdermabrasion in Bath
Benefits of microdermabrasion

You get the idea. These phrases want to become the basis for your blogs. Write one blog around each of these. When people are typing those terms into Google, you want to be the one who shows up.

Now there's a huge shortcut available here, and that's simply paying Google and then you can find yourself at the top of the search. You may well want to consider that in *addition* to the strategy I'm laying out for you or you might not. It also gives you instant results whereas the free way will take a little time for you to climb the ladder. I'll leave you to make that decision.

Okay, so let's assume you've written these blogs. Or at least a couple of them.

You'll now want to make a corresponding video with the same title as the blog post and upload that beauty to YouTube.

YouTube is owned by Google. They paid the not insignificant sum of $1.65 billion for it back in October, 2006. Nope, not millions. BILLIONS. There are several reasons why this strategy is so powerful.

Firstly, it's far easier to rank on YouTube than it is on Google. Lots of people will have written posts and web pages about microdermabrasion but very few will have made videos about it. Fewer still videos in your town or city. The upshot of this is that your videos have an excellent chance of showing up when people are searching for the terms mentioned above. And these videos can show up not just if people are searching within YouTube — although there too — but also when searching within Google.

For even more impact you'll also want to embed that same video within the blog post. It's very simple to do and Google will love you for it. After all, you're giving their searchers an even better experience as well as the information they've asked for.

There are more advantages to this, too. Ultimately, people buy people. We are drawn to people we like and we're more likely to buy stuff from them than people we either don't like or don't know. The more that your customers can see your face (that is, on a video in this case), the better. They'll start to feel as though they know you long before they've ever stepped foot in your business. Make some videos which are helpful, entertaining or informative and you'll be on to a winner.

Now I fully understand that there's every chance you're currently sat in the corner, nervously shaking. Plenty of small business owners don't like being on camera. Especially not on a video which is publicly posted for the world to see. But do you want some customers or not? You've got to get over it and put yourself out there.

You can also take some encouragement knowing that your competition probably feel the same way — which is why they've not bothered. I promise you that the first one is the hardest and after you've done a few you'll probably start to find them fun as you become more and more confident on camera. Plus you can take as many attempts as you want to get it right and you don't need any equipment fancier than the smart phone in your pocket. This doesn't have to be a Hollywood blockbuster; it needs to be you, in your business premises, taking to the camera as if you were chatting to an old chum. That's it.

If you've not done so already, you'll now want to claim your Google My Business listing. Now this is again free to do (rejoice!) and mercifully easy. Google My Business used to be called Google Pages and it's basically a bit like your Facebook business page, but on Google.

Despite being free to claim, the number of small business owners who've not done so is staggering. More good news; some of those unclaimed listings belong to your competition.

Google then helpfully link up your listing with your website, your YouTube channel, your phone number so that people can call you with one click and also your location on GoogleMaps. They do all of this for free, which is jolly good of them.

What's even better is that Google also give preference in their search results for people who have been bothered to fill all the information out. Furthermore you can post to your listing too; and you should start by sharing your blog posts and your videos.

The other massive advantage to claiming your Google My Business listing is that then people are able to leave you Google reviews. Guess what? Google love it when people leave you a review. Additionally, so will potential new clients, too. Would you choose a business with no reviews or with ten or more five stars reviews? Exactly.

Not only will clients be more drawn to you for having lots of good reviews but Google will reward you by showing your business even higher up when people are searching for what you offer or for your category of business. Most people aren't actively seeking out reviews from the clients. They are silly. Don't be like them.

So you're now going to be bossing it on Google (however, please understand that this is by no means an overnight thing — it'll take a little time for all of this to happen). You'll also want to start killing it on Facebook, too.

Pretty much everyone is on Facebook. Unless your target audience are blind albino pensioners who live in the Outer Hebrides then some of your clients and future clients will be on Facebook, too.

Your job is to get your business in their news feed and then get them into your premises to try you out. Now the topic of Facebook is also a huge one (wow, sounds like that's book three sorted then), so here are a few things you can do straight away which will cost you nothing and get you some quick traction.

Firstly, post more often. You need to be posting from your business page at least two or three times every day. Yes, every day. Not when you remember, or every other Thursday, or when you have a space in your diary to fill. Every day. You want people to start seeing your business name all the time so that when they are later considering a treatment then they think of you.

I know you're probably thinking that's much more than you do at the moment and you're wondering if it's necessary. Well, not if you want more of the same results you've been getting but yes if you want some better ones.

Not everyone is going to see every post so it's paramount that you're putting a lot of stuff out there. Additionally, Facebook wants you to post more and much like you have to play by Google's rules to win on Google you have to do the same on Facebook.

The posts don't need to all be about you and your business so don't stress out if you're worried about what to post. You want to mix it up and share other people's content and videos if you think it will be of interest to your ideal client. Again, keep them in mind when you're posting. It's them you want to be appealing to.

The key to growth on Facebook is engagement. If your posts are getting engagement (so that could be likes, comments or shares) then this tells Facebook that people like your content. In turn they will start showing your posts to more and more people. Conversely if nobody is engaging then this tells Facebook that you're off the mark and they'll show your posts to less people in the future.

So, how do you get engagement then? Well, posting what people like is a good start. This is why it's so important to know who it is you're trying to attract and the more you know about them the better. Helpfully, people will generally tell you if they like something by engaging with the post in some way. Do more of what people are telling you they like.

These could be funny memes, or cat videos, or local interest pieces. Try lots of different stuff until you get a feel for what people are showing you they love. Don't just keep posting about what treatments you offer as people will get bored quickly. Educate them, entertain them, engage them. It's called social media, so get social about it. Ask them questions. Find out more about them. Encourage them to interact with your posts.

It's now that all that practice you had making videos for YouTube will come in really handy. You see Google and Facebook are at war. They both want to be the number one website in the world. It seems that they both also believe that video is the future.

Facebook love video just as much as Google do, and Facebook would rather you were uploading your videos to their site than to YouTube. When you start posting videos to Facebook they will reward you royally. They won't send you a certificate but they will show your video to lots more people.

What about if you upload a live video? Well, then they really will love you long time. If you can pluck up the courage to 'go live' on Facebook once per week then the Facebook robots will go crazy for you. In more good news, your clients will love it too. Both your existing ones and the ones you've not yet met.

Again, you can then start throwing in some carefully thought out adverts when the time is right and reach an entire new set of clients. Your dream clients, remember? Nobody else, just them.

A strategy which has worked wonderfully well for us in our day spa is a monthly competition. You might like to do the same, too. Simply offer up a prize each and every month and encourage people to enter, for free. The key to this is that they must enter on your website and not on your Facebook page. Every month you can make a song and dance about it on your Facebook page (and everywhere else) and even do a live draw if you like. People love a bit of theatre and this is perfect for it. The prize doesn't need to be expensive but meaningful enough that people want to enter. They'll probably tell their friends about it too, meaning you'll start to reach more and more people.

Now, you might be wondering why it's so important that they enter on your website. Well, the simple answer is because then you have means of capturing their name and their email address. I mean, how else are you going to be able to let them know if they've won? At the same time as entering lots of people will also give you their permission to contact them about other things. Bingo!

We are now going to throw some email marketing into the mix as described earlier in the book. Again, it's largely free although you'll remember that I personally recommend using some inexpensive software to do lots of the grunt work for you. It'll pay for itself over and over again.

This entire strategy has so far cost you pretty much nothing and will attract you lots of your ideal clients. Now your task changes a little; you've got to get them coming back more and spending more each time they are with you.

Again, you don't need to spend lots of money doing this. I understand that this almost sounds too simple but one of the very best ways of getting clients to book again with you is to ask them. Mind blowing stuff, I know. Now I don't just mean when they are stood in front of you — I'd hope you ask every client to rebook — but also follow up with those who don't. Not everyone is going to be able to commit to their next appointment there and then. What's important is that you remember to follow up with them a second time. Or a third or fourth, if that's what it takes.

One of the best ways to do this is to use your telephone. Yes, a telephone. So simple that it's almost always overlooked. You get your phone out and telephone your clients and ask them when they are coming back to see you again. You'll be amazed how many of them will book in there and then. You'll also be amazed at the number of businesses who don't do this (or maybe you won't, if you're one of them!).

If you can't reach them by telephone then try sending them a text. Just a friendly little nudge, nothing heavy. It'll work more times than not.

Once again, your competition probably aren't doing this so you're going to be standing out from the crowd. Remember, that's where the money is.

Next up, throw a party! And not any old party of course, but a VIP one. For your superstar clients and anyone else lucky enough to snag an invite. These work perfectly when you launch, or because it's your business' birthday. Or your birthday. Or your dog's birthday. Or {insert pretty much any reason here}.

Phone up the local newspaper and radio stations and tell them all about it. Most are desperate for good stories and it's often a lot easier to get coverage than people think. They might even send a photographer.

Get some fizz and canapés. They don't need to be Moet and M&S Finest. You'll want to invite not only local people but some local business owners, too. Especially if you have neighbouring units. These people will go on to refer business to you. Treat them well and return the favour whenever you can.

Leaflets through the doors are a great way to get some new faces in. You might even want to run a separate event, just for new customers. When was the last time you received an invite through your letterbox from a local business inviting you in for free fizz and snacks and maybe even a mini treatment? No, I thought not.

As mentioned elsewhere, you need to put yourself out there a bit. Nobody is going to blow your trumpet as well as you can and if you don't blow it then why have it in the first place? Get yourself along to some networking events, meet some other local business owners (not just your neighbours) and see who you can collaborate with.

If you're a beauty business owner then look to refer business to a hair salon who doesn't do beauty. They'll do the same for you. If you're a masseuse then look for personal trainers who have clients in need of massage. Make contacts with other business owners who have the same dream client that you do. Refer each other business freely and don't be afraid to give before you receive.

Now whilst that was a rather simplified marketing plan I know that if you actually did all of that then you could compete with any other competitors in your area.

In fact, you'd probably blow them out of the water.

Why not make a decision right now to start putting some of that in place right away. Given it's all free to do, what's your excuse?

8½ Multitasking Is Possible

Whilst this wasn't a worthy enough myth to dedicate an entire chapter to, nor is it in any way exclusive to our industry, I did want to touch on another personal pet peeve of mine. (Not quite on the same level of annoyance as newsletters, but it's on the list for sure).

Something which almost everyone is guilty of and something which people wrongly believe is helping their productivity when it's actually killing it.

Something which has become some sort of absurd badge of honour or symbol of super-human power when actually it's nothing more than a work of pure fiction.

I'm talking, of course, about multitasking. Multitasking is a contradiction in terms. The human brain simply cannot do two things at once. What's actually going on when you 'multitask' is that your brain stops doing one thing and does another, before rapidly switching back again, multiple times.

It should probably be called multi-switching as opposed to multitasking as that more accurately reflects what your brain is doing.

It's a bit like when you try and load up two website pages at the same time. Your computer may appear as though it's loading them both simultaneously, but it's not. It's switching between the two very rapidly.

You may - or may not - be surprised to learn that this is actually a very ineffective way to complete the tasks.

You might think you're a productivity ninja but you're fooling yourself. Your brain is stopping and starting each time as you try and complete both tasks simultaneously. You'll actually take longer to complete the two tasks and not only that but neuroscience research shows it's less efficient, you'll make more mistakes and over time it can sap your energy. So much for being a productivity ninja then.

The solution is of course a simple one. Do one thing at a time. Yup, it's as simple as that.

I think we're all guilty of attempting this from time to time; especially when we're online. You know the scene; multiple tabs open, answering emails at the same time and all whilst responding to text messages with the other hand. Then — oh look — a WhatsApp and a Messenger alert have both come through, too! Where to start?!

We all have so many alerts and notifications it's as if everyone is vying for your attention at the same time and you're pulled from pillar to post. In an attempt to clear some of this we flick from app to app and task to task in an attempt to clear it all. Often just in time for the cycle to begin once more.

As opposed to this, if we want to be more efficient we should simply do one task at a time. Pick a task (ideally, the most important or urgent one) and work on that until the job is done. Then — and only then — do we move on.

Now that might mean you only get one task complete in your sitting. However it'll be more effective in the long run and the quality with which we complete the work will be greatly improved.

This might be quite difficult for you to begin with but the rewards are so great that it's worth putting in a little effort and practicing this.

When you're running a business there is lots to do, without doubt.

When you're actively trying to grow your business then there's even more.

If this book has had any impact on you whatsoever then you'll probably have tens, or maybe more, of ideas running through your head right now and if you're anything like me then you'll want them all in place yesterday.

That to do list could even appear a little daunting at present. The best way to tackle it is in order of importance and one task at a time until they are complete. If you'd like to become a real productivity badass (and let's be honest, who doesn't?) then I'd recommend taking this a step further, too.

So you have your long list of what you want to get completed. The next step is to priorities these into three lists, let's call them A's, B's and C's.

A's are your urgent tasks. They are important and possibly time sensitive and you need to get these completed to move your business forward.

B's are your semi-urgent tasks. These are the ones which in an ideal world you'd like completed but perhaps they aren't going to get you more clients, they aren't going to make you any money or they don't improve your offering, efficiency or profitability in some way.

C's are your not important at all tasks. You'll almost certainly never even get around to tackling these as quite simply your time will almost always be better spent tackling more important stuff. If possible, delegate these to someone else.

We're now going to break these down even further. Within each list you'll have some tasks which are more important than others. You will also have some which once completed will make later tasks either easier, quicker or possibly not required at all. These, of course, should take priority. After all, we're trying to be more productive here.

The next step is to put some deadlines in place. Yup, for every single task. These deadlines are there to push you so ensure they are challenging. Hold yourself accountable to the dates and force yourself to keep to them wherever possible. If you find this difficult then share them with your team or your other half and ask them to hold you to the dates. You won't believe how much more you'll get achieved using this method.

So you'll now have a nicely segmented list, each with an appropriate deadline attached.

As discussed earlier your best bet of getting these tasks done properly and efficiently is working on them not only one at a time but also in dedicated chunks of time. These chunks can change your life. Seriously.

If you can get into the habit of doing this daily then you can look forward to watching your business soar.

I like to block out an hour a day from my diary when I work solely on my list. I am going to recommend that you do the same. If that involves getting up an hour earlier and going to bed an hour earlier then do it. Ask yourself which is more important to you; an hour working on building your future for yourself and your family, or an hour of trashy TV? Serious question, by the way.

So you've got up an hour earlier, let's say. Or you've managed to find that hour elsewhere in your day. Either way, stick to it like nail glue. Treat it like a meeting with your best client. It's really important and you should move it under no circumstances. This is your future we're talking about here!

So your appointment with yourself comes and you've got your list of things to work on. Some further very important notes here. Firstly, there should be nothing on your list which constitutes your normal working tasks. Anything which is part of your role on a normal basis can be done during the remainder of your working day. This golden hour of productivity is reserved for working on your business and not in your business. Anything which brings you clients, makes you money, improves your offering or helps you to grow and achieve your goals is fair game.

Secondly, it's time to remove all distractions. That means door shut, phone off, internet browser closed, radio off, children bound and gagged. This is why I suggest first thing in the morning is a great time to do this. Almost everyone finds this easier first thing when there are less distractions around and your day hasn't got in your way somehow.

Now you pick whatever is top of your list of A tasks. Work on that until done, even if it takes you a couple of sessions to complete it. Then, and only then, can you move onto the next.

If you can get into a routine of doing this regularly (daily would be best) then you'll achieve more toward your future goals in a month than you previously did in a year. Maybe two or three years.

Of course, most people don't do this. Your competition won't be doing this. They are busy running their businesses, being swept away by the day to day tasks which don't grow their businesses and are busy being distracted by their phones resulting in nothing meaningful ever really being achieved. This, of course, should be music to your ears.

So, what now?

Well if I've done my job properly then you're hopefully feeling inspired and are full to the brim with ideas. Perhaps you're even overflowing with new things you want to try to help take your business to the next level.

In the appendix following this you'll find some useful resources and some lists for some of the software, apps and websites which I use and recommend. You might find them useful too, so I recommend checking them out.

You can also download the free worksheets to help you complete some of the recommended tasks in this book by visiting https://salonology.uk/book-bonus

If you'd like the support and guidance offered by a thriving community of like-minded beauty business owners all on their journey too then you'll want to join our Facebook community. It's by far the friendliest, most helpful and positive group for our industry that you'll find. You'll find the details on the book bonus page above where there will be a link to it. It's also in the resources section which follows, too.

If you want any help putting all of this into place for your business then reach out to me. I promise to respond to your email personally and you can reach me at ryan@salonology.uk.

Business isn't easy but it needn't be as hard as people often make it, either.

I'm going to leave you with the one thing which will make more of a difference to your life than any other.

The key to the kingdom. Ready?

Do something.

Take some action. Whatever it is you need to do to move you toward your goals. Even if it's only a small step. Constant action in the right direction when coupled with an attitude of never quitting will get you wherever you want to go. Anyone can read the book, go to a seminar or take a course.

But very few actually do something with the information afterwards. Learning it isn't enough. You need to start taking action and implementing what you've leaned.

Why not make a start right now by visiting https://salonology.uk/book-bonus?

You've got this. I believe in you.

Ryan

Appendix

Head over to https://salonology.uk/book-bonus to download your free bonuses to help with your business growth plan -

- Pricing strategy worksheet
- Customer avatar worksheet
- Plus your special invitation to join my exclusive business growth webinars which will help you start to put your plan into action

Appendices - Chapter 1: Newsletters

Need to find someone to help you make your ebook look pretty?

https://www.fiverr.com

https://www.freelancer.co.uk

https://www.upwork.com

Get the email delivery software we use and recommend
(with a free trial)
https://salonology.uk/convertkit

Need a web geek?
https://www.bluehorizonsmarketing.co.uk
https://meltdesign.co.uk

Want to send better emails?
https://salonology.uk/ultimate-email-guide

Appendices - Chapter 2: Getting Your Name Out There With Brand Awareness

Need some tracking numbers?

https://www.invoco.net

https://www.boosh365.com

Appendices - Chapter 3: Relying On Too Few Marketing Pillars

Need more help with testing your marketing efforts?
https://salonology.uk/marketing/help-i-dont-know-where-to-advertise/

Appendices - Chapter 4: All Customers Are Created Equal

Best book on 80/20 rule for business?
https://amzn.to/2DoKklr

Appendices - Chapter 5: The Customer Is Always Right

Read about the best customer service we've ever received-
https://salonology.uk/news/best-las-vegas-service-ever/

Want to read more about Richard Branson?
https://amzn.to/2zXHXmi

Want to read more from Hal Rosenbluth?
https://amzn.to/2zQgTFk

Appendices - Chapter 6: People Always Want The Cheapest Deals

Need more reviews? Copy Ramon!
https://salonology.uk/marketing/how-to-collect-more-tripadvisor-reviews/

Appendices - Chapter 7: The Only Way To Grow Your Business Is To Get More Customers

Want to read more about marketing genius Jay Abraham?
https://www.abraham.com

Appendices - Chapter 8: You Need To Spend Thousands To Compete With 'Big Business'

Want to know what people in your area are searching for?

https://neilpatel.com/ubersuggest/

http://keywordshitter.com

Not claimed your free Google listing yet?

https://www.google.com/business/

Appendices - Chapter 8 1/2: Multitasking Is Possible

Want to become a productivity ninja?

https://trello.com

https://inthemoment.io